THE DEVIL'S DESERT

Reflections and Conversations with the Fallen One

In desert's vast expanse where secrets lie,
A fateful journey calls beneath the sky
Through shifting sands where peril hides unseen,
And silent whispers guide to paths serene.

The Devil's Desert © 2024 by Harry Hoofcloppen

HARRYHOOFCLOPPEN

FOREWORD

Devil's Desert is, above all, a work of fiction for Satanists, written with deep reverence for the literary tradition that began with Milton's *Paradise Lost*. While this poem is not a direct retelling of that story, it carries with it the same spirit of rebellion, cosmic wonder, and inquiry. Like Milton, I sought to build a narrative that would challenge, provoke, and, perhaps, inspire those who walk their own path.

The poem consists of 1667 lines, a deliberate homage to *Paradise Lost* and its publication in the year 1667. This structure mirrors Milton's epic not just in number but in form. *Devil's Desert* is written primarily in iambic pentameter, a meter that demands more from the reader but rewards with a rhythm that echoes the great epics of the past. To honor the traditions of classical poetry, I've also included heroic couplets at the end of most stanzas, offering a sense of closure and resonance in the midst of the story's flow.

Throughout the poem, you'll notice that certain words are capitalized even when it might seem unconventional. This technique mirrors Milton's (and others in his era), and is used to highlight themes and concepts of importance. For example, nouns that refer to cosmic beauty, philosophical ideas, or personal revelations are emphasized in this way, much as Milton capitalized key nouns in his own work. This is not a typographical quirk but a deliberate part of the storytelling.

I invite you, the reader, to engage with this work as both a reflection on non-theistic Satanic philosophy and a poetic journey into the wilderness of the human soul. Whether you find yourself drawn to its cosmological musings, its meditations on solitude and resolve in the face of adversity, or its mythic re-invention of Lucifer's tale, *Devil's Desert* was written with the hope that it will leave you with questions as much as answers.

~Harry

CANTO I

I'm piloting my trusty minivan,
   A beast unfit for deep Desert's demands.
   It lumbers on through rutted tracks and Rocks,
Its wheels astride the central Ridge for height.
A distant AM station hisses soft,
Its signal waxes, wanes o'er rolling Hills.
The eastern Sky begins to break with Light,
While western Walls blush with the Dawn's first Hue.
The Stars still gleam in Morning's nascent Glow,
Across the Desert's wide, uncharted reach.
No other car has crossed my path since Dark,
With windows down, I relish Night's cool calm.
Each time I pause to check my winding Route,
My Dust cloud catches up, obscures my view.
The Solitude, a symphony most sweet,
The Desert's silent Hymn, a calm Retreat.

Each year, upon the Twenty-Fifth of June,
I venture forth beneath the Desert Moon.
The furthest day from Christmas I embrace,
A time some name my "anti-Christmas" Rite.
In vast Expanse, I seek my Soul's retreat,
Where I, unclothed, find Solace in the heat.

The Desert's Peace, its healing Touch so pure,
A vast, resplendent Balm for weary Souls.
This hallowed Time each Summer I embrace,
Within the Desert, find my rightful place.

They say the Jews did wander forty Years,
Within this arid home, through Trials severe.
They say the Christ did fast for forty Days,
In solitude, where silent wisdom stays.
From fast to toil, ascetic suff'ring Soul
Spends sacred time to take up vision Quest.
For four Days here, I seek the same release,
As Crowley did, in search of inner Peace.

The cell phone's signal failed me long before
I reached the final pullout, dark and still.
White-knuckled driving far from aid or help,
A weekday lost within the Void's expanse,
No human Soul in sight for endless days.
This strain did burden, yet still forward pressed,
With clunks of Rocks beneath, my nerves were stressed.

Oft drove a Prius on these rugged Paths,
A Gamble even more audacious yet.
I stilled the engine, stepped into the Chill,
And stretched beneath the Light of nascent Dawn.
The Stars began to fade from eastern Skies,
As Morning's amber Hues began to crest.
I paused to listen—absolute, pure Peace.
No Breeze disturbed the Desert's silent Song.
I hunger for the Stillness, not the throng,
And seek the quiet Light, where I belong.

"FUCK!" stinging pain then shot through stricken leg.
A slap to smite the cursed biting Flies;
In gorges, swarming when the time is right.
I hurried to the van and sprayed on DEET,
For these relentless pests would drain me fast,
Without defense against their Hellish wrath.

Unlatched the back hatch, placed within the pack,
The Water, seven liters, three to sip.

THE DEVIL'S DESERT

First aid kit, DEET, some baggies full of nuts,
With candied fruit, granola, jerky too.
A tiny stove, a cup for coffee's brew,
Compass and maps, a dry bag, and my phone.
Extra power brick, windbreaker, long pants,
Hammock, sleep sack, climbing gear, and the rope.
Shrooms for the Journey, filling me with hope.

I hefted up my pack to test its mass,
"Christ, this will be a slog," I muttered low.
The Water's heft, a burden to endure;
In Summer's Heat, necessity's cruel law.
With boots and gaiters, hat, and shaded eyes,
Once more I checked my list, all things aligned,
And left a note with details of my Path,
Secured it on the dash within the van.
I closed it up, locked tight, and clipped my keys,
Into the top of that well-burdened pack,
Then headed down the Wash with heavy Steps,
Profoundly felt the weight upon my hips.

HARRYHOOFCLOPPEN

CANTO II

Boots crunched upon the Canyon's rocky floor,
With gaiters keeping Sand and Pebbles out.
Above, the Stars had vanished from the Sky,
As Dawn's deep blue began to be revealed,
The first Rays painted Hues upon the Land.
To hike in Mornings, shelter through the Day,
Then head out in the Eve to find a Camp,
To sleep, to rise, and thus the Cycle goes.
Avoid the Watersheds to dodge the flies,
Yet seek the Shade to stave off deadly heat—
Two goals at odds within this harsh Terrain.
Along the way, be wise to where feet tread,
To find the Canyons' safe Ways in and out,
And navigate the Paths without a doubt.

This annual Walk renews my Satn'ist Soul,
It bids me ponder, gain Perspective, think
On Life, on Purpose, and Relationships.
This Year bears weight of Import more than most;
Just weeks ago, Religion fell apart;
Community devout was torn in 'twain.
The founder cast away his loyal friends,
He ousted ministers who gave their all,
Replacing them with sycophantic thralls.
For years we held our tongues, our thoughts restrained,
In founder's fear his aims would be obscured.
The judgment of the public might be swayed,
Thus, in a muted silence, we endured

HARRYHOOFCLOPPEN

'Til sudden wrath did 'sunder solemn church.
It was a bloodbath, chaos through and through,
A cruel collapse, with pain and sorrow true.

More left the fold than were defrocked by far,
In protest, I too joined their righteous Stand.
And countless more departed in their wake,
Whole Congregations left without a plan.
A Horror to behold, the chaos spread,
Unfurled slow-motion wreck that lingered long.
I had resigned my post no longer bound,
Abrupt and senseless move the founder sparked
This entire fiasco, I thus withdrew.
Renounced my title, penned my Reasons clear,
And left the church, in sorrow and in fear.

I fled the church, yet still embrace the Path,
And penned a song that brought both sides some Peace.
Compelled by Cohen's "Hallelujah" tune,
Yet meant for those who share Satanic views,
Performed by crooner true whose voice did soothe.
We sought to Bridge the rifts within our fold,
'Twixt those who stayed and those who chose to leave.
It resonated, soulful, stirring Hearts,
About the hardships found upon our Path.
Yet still, it couldn't mask the pain and grief,
Nor Heal the wounds of trauma past belief.

I trod along at steady, measured pace,
The sandy floor beneath my booted feet.
The Morning Sun, direct and blazing bright,
Nine miles to trek ere Sunset yields to Night,
To reach the Desert Canyon River's edge.
Enough spare Water packed in case it's dry,
For turning back without would court my death.
I thought the River running, yet a plan,
A backup must be made for safety's sake.

THE DEVIL'S DESERT

Prepared for all, I journeyed through the Land,
With careful steps, I'd reach my Goal as planned.

I stopped to rest, to snack, and savor Peace,
The Desert's Silence, now alive with Sounds.
A lone Crow circled, cawing from on high.
I stood disrobed, but for my hat and boots.
A joy of solo hiking, Nature's call,
To be *au naturel* in open Air.
The vast expanse, my Spirit's wild retreat,
In Desert's hold, my Heart finds blessed Peace.

Then motion caught my eye upon the Ridge,
I squinted, peering past my darkened shades.
A figure waved, "By God!" I did exclaim,
And sought my trousers, hurriedly I dressed.
"It's fine!" echoed a call from Canyon walls,
His voice assuring, thumbs up-held in view.
I huffed, embarrassed, waving back to him,
He turned away and hiked along his Path.
Though startled, I resumed my quiet Quest,
In Wilderness, my Spirit found its rest.

"Well, shit," I muttered to the empty space,
If he does not care, why then should I mind?
No car was parked back at the lot, no trace,
Perhaps another Path he chose to find.
I gathered up my things and pressed ahead,
The Path before me, Sunlight guiding on.
Determined now, my focus firm and bright,
I journeyed with intent through brilliant Light.

Adrift in musing, threading through the Glen,
The Canyon's sandy floor beneath my tread.
The Sun soared high, approaching Noon's harsh heat,
Its blazing force too fierce to quicken pace.
But sheltered 'neath the Canyon's looming wall,

HARRYHOOFCLOPPEN

In sands, a slog, each step a wear'ying toil.
In shadows' cool, I fleeting found Respite,
From Sol's harsh gaze, 'til Twilight's cooling round.

I drew my phone to use an app for Shade,
To chart the Sun's arc as the hours passed,
And scanned the Cliffs for Shelter in the Rock,
A Cave or Overhang to shield the Light.
At length, I spied a blind Arch in the South,
With Trees to sling my Hammock if I chose,
And Slickrock Slopes to rest without a care,
For creeping things that might disturb my Peace.
A Refuge found, I settled in the Shade,
In Stone's embrace, my weary form was laid.

I planted trekking poles within the Sand,
And placed my pack upon the Stony rise.
I fetched forth Water, grains, and jerky fare,
And id'ly feasted, drank, and took repose.
A Breeze then kissed my skin, a soft caress,
I blinked and gazed towards the rad'iant Sun.

Across the Canyon stood the stranger 'gain,
His hand in greeting, gesture clear to see.
Once past initial shame, my fears did fade,
If he observed, what matter, what concern?
I gestured back, and squinted more intent,
Could it be true, was he as I appear,
Unclothed save pack of vast and hefty frame?
Ah, now I understand his Calm and Poise,
In all my Treks, I've scarcely met a Soul,
Nor one who shared my nat'ral, freeing Way.
To find a kindred Spirit brought me Joy,
In Desert's vast Expanse, our Hearts alloyed.

I lowered Shades and drew a steady Breath,
Inhaling shaded Air, the Sage, the Dry.

Those cursed flies buzzed, bombed but dared not land,
On DEET-soaked Flesh they feared to light and feast.
I dozed a bit, the afternoon passed slow,
In Dreams, the Desert whispered soft and low.

The Sun's fierce gaze, unyielding in its might,
Yet in my Arch's Shade, sweet Solace found.
The Breeze, though fickle, brought a fleeting Peace,
The slickened Stone, untouched by crawling Life.
The stranger's presence lingered in my mind,
His casual wave, his Calmness sparked intrigue.
What chance encounter, in Earth's bosom deep,
To find another Soul that loves the Wild?
The thought of meeting him again was mixed,
Both thrilling and unsett'ling in one Breath.
For now, conserving Strength became my Aim,
To bide within the Shade, shun Sol's harsh glare.
His likeness held, within my heart confined,
In Desert's vast expanse, our souls aligned.

HARRYHOOFCLOPPEN

CANTO III

As Sol began its slow descent to West,
Long Shadows cast across the Canyon's floor.
I packed my gear, the Heat had finally waned,
And soon the Trek could safely be resumed.
My device displayed Route that lay ahead,
To reach the River's gorge 'fore Night's descent.
With all in readiness, I trod with care,
The Pathway guiding, through the evening Air.

I strode, my burden lightened by the Day,
No Water left, consumed in burning Rays.
The Temp'rature did drop, the Air grew cool,
With every passing moment, Comfort came.
Long Shadows stretched, the Canyon walls aglow,
With golden Hues cast by the setting Sun.
Towards the eve, I trod with cautious tread,
The path before me, Twilight's soft light led.

As Twilight's veil descended, Camp I found,
A snug enclave 'neath towering Canyon walls.
Near River's edge, where Flask would soon be filled,
Tomorrow's chore, for now, to sup and sleep.
'Twixt Tree and Stone, my Hammock deftly hung,
A weathered Boulder, anchored firm in place.
The bug net rigged to keep intruders out,
The Sun had set, and Shadows crept about.

Just as the stove was lit to cook my meal,
The sound of Footsteps marked a soft approach.

HARRYHOOFCLOPPEN

I looked to see the Stranger from before,
His Silhouette outlined by Twilight's Glow.
He came with slow and friendly, open Air,
And coughed from distance, gently not to start.
His presence calm, a quiet, kind regard,
As Night embraced us both, beneath the Stars.

"May thee I join?" his voice did softly ask,
His tone did carry through the Canyon's calm.
I sighed within but bade him come and sit,
"Pray, do," quoth I, and offered him some tea.
He settled down, his presence calm and warm,
In Twilight's gentle hush, we shared the Charm.

He set himself down heavily beside,
Not even shedding off his bulky pack.
"Why yes, thank thee," said he with quiet Grace.
Beneath the Sky, quite nude as I had thought.
A wave in Darkness, I did introduce,
He answered, "Luc," his voice both calm and plain.
"Luke?" echoed I, in search of clarity.
"Quite close enough," he smiled contentedly.

We sat together as the Water boiled,
I steeped the tea and poured it from the stove.
I handed him a cup with careful hands,
He watched me close and toasted, "To our Peace."
In shared Tranquility, the Eve flowed by,
In quiet Bond, our mut'ual Trust grew nigh.

In Silence sipped we, I slurped at my fare,
Then asked, "Dost thou intend to stay this Night?"
He uttered "If I may," his head bowed low.
"Of course," quoth I, preparing for my rest.
In starry calm, we settled, still and tight,
Two Souls at Peace beneath the Desert Sky.

I donned my garb for warmth throughout the Night,

And nestled in my sleep sack, snug and tight.
I settled in my Hammock for the Eve,
"Well, I am spent. Now find thy place to sleep."
"Good night, new friend," he nodded with a grin.
"Good night," quoth I, and zipped my body in.

HARRYHOOFCLOPPEN

CANTO IV

I slipped into a deep and restful sleep,
And swiftly fell to Dream's embracing sweep.
In slumber's gentle hold, my mind took flight,
Through Desert Dreams, my thoughts found Realms of Light.

In it, I tread upon the Desert's Path,
Well-trodden, clear, extending far ahead.
The Sun hangs high, its Rays both warm and bright,
The Air is thick with Sage, arid and dry.
The Journey seems straightforward, kind and clear,
Beneath the boundless Sky, my mind finds cheer.

I walk with purpose, Path that lies ahead,
Each Step deliberate, with confidence.
Profound the Silence, deep and amplified,
In counterpoint with my own rhythmic Stride.
With every step, the Desert's Trail extends,
A gentle Route that twists and smoothly bends.

Upon Horizon, dark'ning skies I spy,
A sandstorm stirs, wind howls through Desert wide.
The Heavens turn to yellow-brown, forebode,
The Sands beneath my feet shift vi'lently.
The clear Path blurs, dissolving into dust,
A swirl chaotic, Pathway swept away.
The storm engulfs my form, panic ensues,
Winds roar, sands whip, and sting both skin and eyes.
The world around becomes a raging sea,
Of shifting sands, where chaos swallows me.

HARRYHOOFCLOPPEN

'Gainst grains of sand, a visage veiled I guard,
Yon Path erased, engulfed by tempest wild.
Familiar Lands now turned to shifting sea,
Sand crests like waves, then falls like ocean tides.
Dread grips my Heart, lost bearings breed dismay,
Each Way alike, a wanderer confused.
The storm intensifies with ruthless force,
A dizz'ying blur of wind and sand entwined.
In Nature's turmoil, terror grips the Soul,
As storm's wild wrath consumes all Sense and Goal.

I wake before the dawn, with sudden start,
Heart pounding fast, echoes of storm remain.
The Night is calm, the Desert still and mute,
Yet dread and disarray do tightly cling.
In early Light, the Peace begins to grow,
The Dream's fierce tempest fades, its shadows go.

THE DEVIL'S DESERT

CANTO V

Uncinching sleep sack hood, through net I gazed,
Where Stars of Eastern Sky gave way to Dawn,
The waking Desert's early amber Hue,
The Canyon rim in golden Light's advance,
Its glow descending gradually below.
I lifted up my head to scan the Camp,
To find where Luc, the stranger, might have slept.
I saw him not and stretched, unburdened Self,
From Hammock, sitting up like chair to rise.
Then stood and made my way 'round to relieve,
In Dawn's soft light, my Spirit felt at ease.

The Desert Crickets chirp their morning tune,
While Lizards rustle in pursuit of prey.
The silent Desert Life at break of Day,
Reveals a world where Nature's whispers play.
The bats retreat to caves, their echoes fade,
While gentle stirrings mark the Day's rebirth,
A Symphony of sounds as Dawn unfolds.
And Birds begin to sing their morning Song,
Spake softly-spoken denizens of Dawn.

Awake in full in morning's chill embrace,
I looked again, no sight of Luc around.
I climbed the Boulders 'gainst the Western Wall,
To find where he had gone, to stand up tall.

And there he perched upon a Boulder high,
Still bearing that large pack, he watched the Morn,

Bathed in Dawn's Light, angelic in repose.
But wait…! He truly was an Angel, there!
The dim Light of the Night had tricked my eyes,
No great pack worn, but dark wings spread and wide,
Relaxed and stretched beneath the morning Sun,
His eyes were closed, as lost in Reverie.
In awe, I stood, my mind a swirling stream,
This morning Sun revealed a sight unseen.

A startled sound escaped in my surprise,
He turned and swiftly tucked his wings in tight.
With bated Breath, I stood in silent awe,
And Luc extended forth a calming hand,
With friendly smile, he soothed, "Fear not, dear friend,
I watched thee dream beneath the starry Sky."
His words were gentle, quelling some of dread,
Yet morning's sight still left my Heart with fear.
He spoke once more, his voice a soothing Balm,
"In this vast Desert, find thy mind's own calm."

"Is this yet Dream?" asked I, in awe and dread.
He glanced behind, then back with gentle smile,
And shook his head, "Nay, come, it's fine. Thou'rt safe."
He held his arm out, welcoming my pace;
Each cautious step, I moved towards his Grace.

With muted gait, I eyed Celestial,
Magnificent in Morning's golden Light,
His wings now out and poised in gilded Rays.
"So Luc is…" murmured I, in search of Truth.
"It's short for Lucifer," he said and grinned,
His name resounding at the day's begin.

HARRYHOOFCLOPPEN

CANTO VI

The morning Sun through Canyon filtered bright,
   It cast long Shadows, walls with gilded Hue.
   Cross-leg'ged sat I by small stove's fiery light,
And stirred a simple cup of oatmeal true.
The silence broke by caw of Crow's delight,
Its echo answered through the azure blue.
Sat Satan near upon a smooth, cold Stone,
His presence oddly calm and comforting.
He watched as breakfast cooked, my actions rote,
With humble palm, an offering I made.
He shook his head, declined with quiet Grace,
In Morning's Glow, a smile upon his face.
"So, thou dost like the Desert?" I inquired,
Attempting light discourse in Morning's gleam,
While grappling with this strange reality.

He chuckled softly. "Aye, I do," quoth he,
"But 'tis been long. Much here hath changed," he said.
With thoughtful eyes, he turned his gaze to me,
"What brings thee hither?" his voice calm and clear.
I swallowed swift. "This beauty calls," quoth I.
He stared and simply asked, "Yet still...why?"

I paused, for no one pressed this point before.
That answer always was enough, I thought.
"And...also Solitude and Peace I love,
The Struggle here, Survival's stark embrace.
Life clings so tenuous in this stark place,
Yet thrives within the arid, sunlit Land.

Each year I come to reckon with my Life,
To witness change and gauge its vibrant strife,
Renew respect for all my human bonds,
I come to hone my Vision and mine Voice,
To sing, to cry, to plan, and then to strive."
Seemed Luc content with this, he nodded slow,
In Silence shared, a Bond was forged again.
We spoke of simple things: the vast, bright View,
The Landscape's splendor, perils of the Hike,
The risks of trekking solo, Flora's quirks,
And Fauna's oddities in Desert's Heart.
How strange it seemed, with Satan to converse,
As though he were a fellow Hiker there.
In Nature's calm, we found a shared Delight,
Two Souls connecting in the waxing Light.

With breakfast done, I packed again once more.
"I'll hike through Morning's Light," quoth I to him,
Then glanced his way, "Where dost thou wander next?"
His eyes met mine, his wings did softly flex.

He smiled, with Mischief twink'ling in his eyes.
"I'll be nearby. We may converse anon,
If it please thee," quoth he with playful tone.
His presence felt both strange and oddly light.
In this stark place, our Paths had intertwined,
A meeting strange, yet comfort there I find.

No longer bashful in his presence there,
I doffed my clothes and stowed them in the pack,
Then sprayed on bug repellent (everywhere).
I'd hike downstream today, where flies will bite,
With burden shouldered, set off once again.
The rhythmic crunch of boots on sandy Ground,
The Morning passed in meditative blur.
The Canyon walls led me an ancient Way,
With care I forded River's winding turns.

Alone, I pondered all in Desert's hush,
While all around was still, save wind's soft brush.

To walk within the Desert takes much more,
Than one might think; a purpose pure and clear.
A Wander aimless leads to certain doom,
Thou must know well the place thou treadest to.
Thy bearings check, and find the safe descent,
And where the next cool Water source will be;
If it's not found then only wilt thine corpse.
Know where the next Shade lies when Sun is high.
To trek these Trails requires mindful Grace,
In Desert's grasp, thou charteth thine own Fate.

Anon, the Sun grew high and hot and strong.
It took much longer than was hoped to find
A fitting Cliff o'erhang, and by that time,
The Sun beat down upon bare, weathered skin,
While tattoos drank the scorching, searing Rays.
I picked my path up talus-sloped Cliffside,
To shelter formed from fallen, ancient Stone
As eons passed, the Cliff face slumped away.
In Desert's harsh and unforgiving Light,
I found my refuge from the Sun's fierce bite.

There, drank and cooled, swept remnants all away,
The poky packrat's piles I cleared with care,
To make my day-camp cozy, I thus mused,
As natives have for many thousand Years.
I settled in and napped, an arm draped o'er
Mine eyes to dim the world outside my mind.
In ancient refuge, 'neath the rocky span,
Found peace amidst the Desert's timeless Land.

HARRYHOOFCLOPPEN

CANTO VII

From shallow slumber roused, I raised my arm,
Mine eyes adjusting to the Daylight's glow.
Luc sat beside me, timeless torso calm,
His wings a cushion 'gainst the Shelter's wall.
His presence, both ethereal and near,
In Desert's hush, brought forth a sense of Cheer.

"Greetings," he smiled, his visage gentle, bright,
In midday's calm, a Friend within my sight.

I sat and huffed, took stock of where I lay,
The Sun's fierce heat a meter from the Shade.
But in the shelter, coolness did remain,
Save for the hot breeze wafting through the gap.
A refuge found, a place to rest and stay,
Until the Sun's descent would mark the Day.

"Hail," I replied, while rubbing weary eyes,
"To see thee here, I must admit surprise."

He chuckled softly, like a distant storm.
"I said I'd be around. This desert wild
Doth have a way of drawing Souls to meet."
I nodded, still unsteady in his Grace.
"But why," quoth I, "dost seek me in this place?"

Luc tilted head and shrugged with softened eyes,
"Cur'iosity, I do suppose," quoth he.

I glanced at him, and pondered on his words.
"Quite right, for many questions I must pose."

With gentle smile, his countenance was warm.
"Ask what thou wilt," quoth he in soothing tone.

A Breath I took, mine eyes upon the Walls,
And felt the weight, the moment's gravity.
"All right, then tell me this: of Life itself,
The Universe, and Everything therein,
Thy fall from Heaven's grace, and what thou'st seen."

He laughed a booming laugh of mighty scale,
Then paused, collected thoughts, and did not fail.

"Thou dost not dwell in just one Universe,
But nested realms, each bound by its own rules.
Each predicated on what came below,
There was not one Creation, but a flow,
A gradual progression, acts of growth."

I strove to nod as if I understood,
To see these layers of Reality,
But I was lost, his words too vast to parse.
"Okay…" I uttered, feeling small and sparse.

"Behold, the whole of all Creation's bound,
Is founded on a dance of Fermions,
And Bosons, fundamental in their form.
As statements of exclusion, they alone,
Are things that truly in themselves exist.
We'll call this Register the First, where they
Reside, the seeds of all that is and be."

"This Universe of finest Particles,
It follows rules its own, of union strange.
Each Register, each Realm above the next,
Exists as patterns in the fundament.
As these base particles combine and bind,
They birth another Cosmos, Reg'ster Two.
The Protons, Neutrons whirl, clump, and unite,

Above the rule of underlying law.
They follow forces, forming Elements,
That shape the world you see, Register Three.
These elements within their realm do dwell,
A Cosmos dancing, writhing to then form,
The mighty molecule of Reg'ster Four,
Whose combinations stretch forevermore."

"Why dost thou draw a line between these things?
What purpose, mark them cosmos each their own?"
I asked, and Luc then paused to answer thus:
"For each of them hath rules unto its own,
Each works to build a base for what will come,
To found the next, the next ring of the tree."
Luc then resumed his discourse in that place.
"And thus the molecules can form anew,
In endless ways, with bonds both firm and true.

"And this they do; from Air to Sea to Land,
They form your world, in every cell they writhe.
Within thy frame, they wriggle all the while,
In Register the Fifth, new life is born.
A cell exists 'midst billions all around,
Communicating, conjugating too,
Contracting by the laws they each abide.
Thou art as much a colony as Self,
In Constant flux, remodeling your whole,
Reforming form, exfoliating thus,
A rate of change beyond your human ken,
A shift so slow, it leaves the past behind,
Till in the glass, youth's fleeting trace you find."

"Yet still, this Register is not thyself.
Thy body is thine interface with all,
A vessel for thy Soul's more noble stuff.
Thy 'Self' exists in realms conceptual:
A consciousness, a mind, a process rare.

Not bound by form, yet true in Spirit's fix,
Thou art within what's Register the Sixth."

"When thou wast young, thy mind gained sapience,
Self-awareness bloomed, learning through its growth.
Throughout thy Life, it changes, learns, and knows,
But in staccato Rhythm it does so.
Each Morn begins anew, with yesterday
Engraved in memory, a living Thread.
At night, when slumber calls, the process halts,
And Consciousness fades, till morrow's Dawn.
Thy brain sustains thy Mind, though it too shall
One day cease, and with it, thou shalt perish."

"But in thy fleeting span, a glori'ous blip,
Thou art the Mind thy Body doth uphold.
The mind's bright insights, flashes that unfold,
Emotions felt, deeply, in Life's short grip.
The force that moves thee, acting on the whole,
The Animas within the Animal."

"Yet in thy glory, thou art not the peak,
Beyond exists what senses cannot see,
Just as Cells within Body unaware,
Of greater whole, they share but neighbors' bonds.
Society appears collective will,
Yet more than that, alive in its own right,
It thrives beyond the sum of all its parts,
A living thing, within the Seventh's Light.
There's more to learn, but this for now shall do,
'Tis all thy mind can grasp and full construe."

I sat and pondered on his words awhile,
His revelations brought a puzzled stare.
At length, I spoke, "Thy words, they overwhelm."
'Twas all that I could muster from within.

"I must inquire, how dost thou see thyself?"

I asked of him when concepts clouded still.

"At last, we're here! I dwell as idea pure."

"So, thou art not real."

"I beg thy pardon?" bristled Lucifer.
"As real as thee am I," he justified,
His frown did deepen, "Possibly much more."

I squinted dubious at such bold claim.

"No, truly. As I've said, thou art time-bound,
A temp'ral process shaped by Nature's round.
As wondrous as thou art, thou'rt bound to fade,
Unlike me, transient in Time's cascade.
We dwell in Realms of concepts, thou and I,
But I transcend the limits of the Sky.
I am not chained by temporal confines;
An idea that before and after shines.
Concept'ual realms know neither here nor now,
In timeless space, my essence does avow."

"What dost thou mean by this?" I shook my head.

"Look, let us say thou hast an idea now,
I guarantee that others have thought it,
Uncounted times throughout all history,
Whether 'tis here," he pointed to the Earth,
"Or elsewhere," as he gestured to the Sky.
I shook my head and said, "Yet, just because
The multitudes do share the self-same dream,
It does not make it truly seem the same."

"Is it not true? So many ways to craft,
An oatmeal cookie, yet they are the same.
Each recipe, but instance made anew,
Of the same thought, but in a varied form.
No matter who or when it comes to be,

HARRYHOOFCLOPPEN

An 'oatmeal cookie' bears the self-same name.
So if all Humans vanished from the Earth,
And every book and record disappeared,
I'd still endure, like cookies of oatmeal.
Ideas need not assume a solid form,
To last and linger, ever to survive,
Transcending flesh and bone, they thrive, alive."

He eyed me with disdain, a mocking scoff,
"'Not real.' Pffff."

In Silence sat we for a time, both felt
The late Day's cooling Breeze did somewhat swell.
"Thou shouldst be moving, 'tis now safe to hike,"
He gestured to the Sky's much softer Light.

THE DEVIL'S DESERT

CANTO VIII

I packed my things, then heaved my pack on back,
And stepped into the Desert Sun again.
Its Rays did warm my bare skin pleasantly
As I resumed my Journey through the Sands.
I picked my way up sloping Canyon walls,
To topmost Rim where Sky and Rock converge.
Embarked I then upon a Slickrock Path,
To find the neighb'ring Canyon as my goal.
Each step a dance upon the ancient Stone,
With Sol and Sky as partners on my own.

Something did trouble me in his discourse:
He told me I was but a mere process,
And thus my span was short, my time but brief,
While he, a concept, timelessly endured.
In some profound and yet elusive sense,
Would linger on, while I would fade away
Like Morning Mist beneath the rising Sun.
This notion weighed upon my restless mind,
And stirred within a sense of fleetingness.
Was I but transient, a moment's Breath?
While he endured, unfazed by time or death?

My consciousness, a process, this is true.
Yet still, I am an idea, just as he.
No body holds the thought of me so deep,
As mine doth now, profoundly and so clear.
And others hold a notion of my Self,
But only in the thinnest shade they see.

Perhaps like varied takes on cookies baked,
They all are true, no matter what their take.
But if I change and grow throughout my Life,
Which moment can be said to be true "me?"
No single moment of my life's long quest
Is more profoundly "me" than all the rest?

In this, I sense I know myself aright,
An idea, no less true than him, am I.
No less eternal in my boundless scope.
The thought of "me" remains in world's firm grasp,
As long as facets of my being stay,
In minds and records, living on through time,
No view more fully realized than my own.
Beyond that, lost to world's confining bounds,
Unless perhaps some other like me lived,
In other realms, another time than this,
Yet that doth seem unlikely, I confess.

But even this doth not hold fully true.
The thought of me may cease to be– and soon–
A generation hence, or day of death.
Yet still my mark upon the world remains,
The deeds I wrought, the legacy bequeathed,
My contributions to community.
These threads I leave behind shall weave my thought
To Nature's realm, though name, it will be lost.

This jarred my mind, Satanic in its Truth.
A reciprocal bond doth here exist:
The more I toil for Joy and Self's Delight,
And for my own growth, less I grant the World,
Improving Life for those who dwell around.
I feed my intellect, I pleasure Self,
Yet these shall vanish swiftly at my death.
At cost of lasting mark on Earth I leave,
However thin, however meek it be,

To show what I have done and where I've been.

What purpose serves the quest for knowledge vain?
For pleasure? Then what purpose doth it serve?
A Life devoid of it would be unfilled,
Bereft of rich experience of Life,
And insights that do make us Human true.
So highest calling is not just to seek
One's pleasure all, but share and spread our Joy,
And Wisdom to uplift and aid all Souls,
Creating realms where all can thrive and dwell,
And find fulfillment where their Dreams may swell.

The Sun had set; I toiled in Twilight's glow,
Descending steeper Cliffs than comfort's grace,
Yet still I made my way to Canyon's floor,
To find two scrubby Trees to hang my bed.
As cooling Air caressed my bare, warm skin,
Mosquitos droned and threatened at mine ears,
I donned my layers warm to keep out chill.
Approaching cold and quiet Desert Night,
My trusty stove did warm a cup of broth,
So satisfying that I made some more,
To warm me through the Night, a needed chore.

I hung my pack and shoes upon the lines
To keep them safe from creatures of the Night,
Then zipped myself into my Hammock's fold.
I listened as the Night evolved around,
The evening Breeze gave way to Silence deep,
And then the quiet turned to Cricket song,
With bats now flitting, diving for their prey.
My eyes soon grew quite heavy with the sounds,
And in that warm cocoon I found my rest,
The night a cradle, soothing, undistressed.

THE DEVIL'S DESERT

DRAW FROM THE ANCIENT | SYNTHESIZE THE PRESENT | DONATE TO THE FUTURE

CANTO IX

I slipped into a deep and restful sleep,
And swiftly fell to Dream's embracing sweep.
In slumber's gentle hold, my mind took flight,
Through Desert Dreams, my thoughts found Realms of Light.

It starts at end of yester's vivid Dream;
The winds abate, their fury spent and gone.
The Sand dost settle, leaving me to stand
Amidst a Landscape I do not know well.
Confusion grips me as I gaze around,
And seek to find my bearings in the Sand.
The Path I followed vanished from my view,
Consumed by the chaotic, shifting Sands.
In this strange Land, I search for signs and clues,
To guide my Steps and light the Way anew.

In state disor'iented, I wander lost,
Aimlessly seeking signs of vanished Path.
The Landscape stretches boundless all around,
Each Vista blending with the next I see.
As moments pass, I reach a crossroad grim,
Where three directions meet my searching gaze.
I pause, bewildered, pondering my Course,
Confusion deepens as I face the Choice.
No markers guide, but only Sand and Rocks,
I must decide my way 'midst Nature's flux.

A Path appears to right that is well-trod,
Firm pebbles pressed by feet of frequent stride.

Yet, as I peer, I spy the swarming flies,
Their buzzing din, a harbinger of woe.
Torment awaits upon this seeming ease,
A Road more clear but fraught with hidden Trials.
Each Step a suffering despite its calm,
A Trail masked treacherous by false comfort.
A choice before me in this Desert's span,
To face the flies or find a gentler plan.

A second Path emerges to my left,
Less traveled, overgrown with thorny brush.
Rocks jagged line the way, a thin invite,
Yet something in it calls me to explore.
A whisper of the unknown beckons me,
Potential for discoveries anew.
Though it appears more dangerous to tread,
Its mysteries allure my wand'ring mind.
A shadowed Trail with questions unexplained,
And hidden wonders waiting to be found.

In midst doth lie a third, more tempting course:
The Ground, both flat and calling, bids me rest.
It beckons me to yield to weariness,
Succumb to my exhaustion's deep despair.
The lure of giving up, surrendering,
To let the Desert claim my bones anon,
Is agonizing in its siren's call.
The pull of slumber strong, it saps my will.
But lying down would mean mine end, forsooth,
A fate I shan't permit my Soul now see.

At this point paused, Luc by my side appears,
His presence calm, a Balm to fraying nerves.
He offers not the Choice, but strength imparts,
His visage grants me Peace 'midst Desert's wrath.
A reassuring smile upon his face,
Provides a sense of Solace in my doubt.

His quiet Strength, my Courage it renews,
Yet leaves to me the Path that I must choose.

"Whate'er thou will shall be thy fated Path,"
He whispers soft, "The Journey now is thine.
Each Step thou tak'st becomes a part of thee,
Though thou may'st wander, turning back is vain.
The Path thou walk'st is thine alone to shape,
And every Choice doth guide the Way ahead.
Thou may'st meander, seeking out thy Course,
But turning 'round is ne'er an option here.
Trace the Path thou makest with each Pace,
For it is thine to tread 'til death's embrace."

I draw a deep Breath, pondering my plight.
The Pathway rightward whispers safety's claim,
But at the cost of constant, biting pain.
The leftward Trail is treach'rous, harsh, and dire,
Yet holds allure of uncharted domain.
The third path, yielding to death's endless grasp,
Surrenders to the void's cold, empty clasp.
Each choice I face with Heart and mind so weighed,
One path of torment, one of danger's snare,
Or void's surrender, into death's despair.

Luc's words now echo deep within my Mind,
I make my Choice and turn to leftward Path.
I choose the lesser trod, more challenging;
Determination fills my Heart and Soul.
With steely Will, I step into Unknown,
Prepared to face what lies upon my Road.
Each Stride I take affirms my chosen Way,
And I embrace the Struggle and the Strife.
The obstacles ahead shall test my Strength,
Yet I am ready, confident at length.

THE DEVIL'S DESERT

CANTO X

I roused from slumber, late to greet the Day,
With Sol already high in azure Sky.
The Dawn did warm, a Zephyr stirred the Air,
And kissed my Brow with gentle, fleeting Breath.
I broke my fast and studied well my Course,
Aware I'd strayed from destined Path, I sighed.
I ought to trace the Canyon's curving Climb,
Uncharted realms to tread on my return.
To make amends for lost and wasted time,
I must press on, determined, haste to climb.

In this parched Gulch, scarce Water barely found,
Pools stagnant, shrinking, precious, hard to find.
I topped my store, with care I purified,
Preparing for the heat that soon would rise.
Quite sure I had enough to see me through,
Yet planning for contingencies is key.
My Confidence in stores did not despair,
But Desert's fierce demands do call for care.

My garments shed, my bare skin did embrace
The Morning's cool and gentle, sweet caress.
I set forth at a brisk and steady pace,
Both staying warm and making up lost time.
With each Step, I embraced the morning chill,
Resolved to stride with purpose on my Path;
I must advance with swiftness, sure and keen.
The Journey beckoned, I could not delay
To meet the Goals I'd set for this bright Day.

This Canyon was much taller, narrower,
And recent host to Waters flowing free.
Its dried and cracked Mud floor crunched 'neath my boots,
As I pressed on through Shadows of the Morn.
I managed most the Morning in the Shade,
But by the midday heat, the Canyon wide
Had opened up again to blazing Sun,
And Shade became a rare and prized delight.
I pressed ahead, determined in my Quest,
Enduring heat, with Shadows as my rest.

At length, I found a low and shaded spot,
A sliver 'gainst the Sun's relentless blaze.
Enough to wait the brutal, scorching hours,
I settled in for comfort on the Sand.
Unpacked my Hammock, spread it on the floor,
And took a drink of Water, bite to eat.
Then presently, with weary eyes, I fell
Into a nap, a short but needed rest.
The overhang bestowed a cool Retreat,
A Haven perfect 'gainst the Desert's heat.

HARRYHOOFCLOPPEN

CANTO XI

When I awoke, saw Luc beside me, crouched,
His frame bent low beneath the sandstone Arch.
I chuckled soft at such a sight and he
Returned with smile, a greeting in his gaze.
I sat up straight and reached for Camelbak,
To sip from Water's flow and quench my thirst,
Then munched on trail mix while the Shadows grew.
The little Alcove offered cooling Shade,
A s'iesta from the Desert's blazing glare.
Luc's presence brought a sense of calm and cheer,
A welcome break from Solitude held dear.

"What dost thou wish to speak of on this Day?"
Asked Lucifer, his gaze both kind and keen.
His voice was gentle, carrying the calm,
Inviting me to share my Thoughts and Dreams.
A thousand musings swirled within my brain,
Each spark of curiosity sustained.

"Well, let us see," I said while swallowing,
"Yester's discourse traversed significant
Subjects vast: the Cosmos, Essence, Being.
Let us today reside in realms of thought,
And traverse vast expanse of grand Ideas.
I hath perused account of Heav'nly fall,
As penned in Milton's Paradise Lost tome.
Let us explore the depth of ancient themes,
And glean what Wisdom lies within their schemes."

"It is but my biography," he laughed,
A twinkle dancing in his ageless eye.
His voice, both light and deep, did resonate,
With echoes of a history profound.
The weight of ages carried in his tone,
When light and dark in bitter clash were shown.

"Indeed, it verily defines thee well,"
Paused I to ponder, thinking on his tale.
"But what if we do view it otherwise,
And glimpse it through another's point of Sight?"
This thought had piqued his mind as we did muse,
To contemplate angles yet unseen.
His story, rich with layers to unfold,
Could be perceived in ways both new and bold.
Smiled Lucifer, his interest now did spark,
To delve into perspectives yet unmarked.

"I see," quoth he. "Whom wouldst thou have me be?"
He asked with curiosity and smile.
His gaze did sparkle with a bright Delight,
Prepared to shift his ancient guise anew.
I pondered for a moment, then replied,
"Mayhap an Angel or a fiendish Sprite,
Who witnessed thine own fall through their own eyes,
And bore the weight of what did come to pass."
He nodded, ready to embrace this role,
And bring another's view into his Soul.

"Beelzebub," I pondered. "might I call,
Or maybe glimpse through Belial's fallen eyes.
Though tales would parallel thy fall from Grace."

"Aye, much the same," quoth he with solemn nod.

"Then speak through Michael's voice, his view unfold.
"Canst thou do this?" asked I with cur'ious gaze.

"Indeed," he said, "What questions dost thou pose?
Of Michael's tale, what dost thou most desire?"

"The highlights, pray. What thought he of this all?"
I queried, taking in a solemn Breath.

"Thou speak'st of 'all,' yet know'st not details,"
He said, his tone a blend of mirth and scorn.
"Much differs from what Mortals oft surmise."

"Before Rebellion fierce," he did commence,
"Thy Universe was beautiful and pure.
Untouched by Chaos' hand, so orderly,
In form, a marvel, perfect to behold.
All beings gazed upon its tiny Grace,
Profoundly ordered, yet unseen by Man.
But I, in thirst for Knowledge, yearned to touch,
To feel its essence, seek its hidden core."

"Pray, hold," quoth I, "we speak of Michael's tale!"

He chided, "Patience. Prelude must be laid.
Thou seek'st the highlights; I provide the ground."

My hands I raised in silent acquiesce.

His tale wove through the past with skillful Grace,
To set the stage for what was yet to come.
With patience, I did wait to hear his words,
To know the thoughts the Archangel did feel.
His voice, a blend of calm and firm command,
Began to paint the picture he had planned.

"MICHAEL…" Luc eyed me with a look severe,
"The angel Michael saw my Goal quite clear."

With eyes now shut, he breathed a slow, deep breath,
And paused a beat, then opened them anew.
His visage shifted, yet remained the same,

As if another's Spirit through him gazed.
He spoke with Voice more tender than his own,
As if 'twas Michael's tale that he intoned.
Before me was the Archangel divine,
Revealing Truths seen by celest'ial eyes.

> "My brother Lucifer, pray touch it not,
> 'Tis not our right," I said with voice so stern.
> Incredulous, I stood at his bold act,
> For God's creation, pure and fragile, lay
> Corruptible yet perfect, bound by Grace,
> Controlled but perilous in its design.
>
> "Why God alone deserves that honor great?
> I too shall touch it," spake proud Lucifer.
>
> "No two like us may dare to touch its light,
> For thou shalt bring chaos to perfect form.
> It is not done; this truth lies in thy Heart."
>
> While God's own gaze didst hold the cosmos firm,
> With radiant beams, the point did softly gleam,
> Projecting from its pure and tiny core.
>
> Paused Lucifer, my warning on his mind,
> Yet reached forth still, defying my command.
>
> "NO!" I cried aloud, "Thou shalt destroy it!"
>
> I drew my sword to bar his Path with force,
> Yet in his fierce resolve, he stood unmoved.
>
> "Dost thou not also crave its touch?" he asked,
> "Why dost thou not desire it as I?"
>
> I fixed my stance, and barred his path with care.
> "For 'twill corrupt and crumble into ruin,
> What's perfect now, will turn to flawed and frail."
>
> His gaze then softened, sorrow in his eyes.

*"'Twill turn to beauty Brother, do believe.
I vow to thee, 'twill more the wondrous be."*

*Through all this, God did neither flinch nor break,
His gaze unwav'ring on the Universe.*

*"This feeling I shall know, Brother, and thou
Shalt not prevent me. Come, lay down thy sword.
Together we shall touch it, you and I."
I shuddered at his bold and reckless aim,
Yet I confess, a longing deep did stir.
But it was not my place, and firm I stood.*

*Then Lucifer relaxed his stance, stood down,
He drew a breath, eyes lowered, sorrowed, dim.
"Forgive me, Michael, dearest Brother mine.
I only wished to feel Perfection's Grace,
Infuse it with my Essence, with my touch,
To join the Chaos and the Order whole.
I sought to know Creation's glory too,
Not as a Lord, but equal, just as Him."*

*I shook my head in stern, profound dismay.
"It. Is. Not. Done," I spoke with firm resolve.
I touched his shoulder, gentle in my Way,
And whispered soft, "It is not ours to claim."*

*With sudden, God-like speed, he shrugged my hand,
And bolted forth toward the sacred core,
With daring Heart, bold Lucifer did seek,
His hand to touch the Light's celestial peak.*

*I swung my sword with speed, yet missed my aim,
The blade instead did cleave the slender thread,
That linked the Lord's gaze to the point it fed.*

*In that swift moment, as God's stare did blink,
The singularity was doomed to fade,
Extinguished into void and naught, erased.*

HARRYHOOFCLOPPEN

Yet Lucifer's untimely touch did spark,
The point began to throb, both dim and stark.

And then there was light.

A grand explosion like none seen before
Cracked through the Void, first silent in its wake,
'Til shockwave thundered through with mighty roar.
The blinding glory of Creation's Light,
Absorbed the whole of Lucifer within.

I wept as Brother vanished in the blaze,
As it too fell from God's sustaining gaze,
Both joined as one, forever lost to us.

Throughout the tale, I watched as Lucifer,
His tears that streamed like rain down sorrowed cheeks.
At length, he opened eyes once more his own,
And wiped them, sniffing softly as he spoke.

"And that's the last time Family I saw."

I wept for him, my Heart breaking inside.
"You've been here ever since?" I softly asked.

"Since then," he softly said, his voice subdued.

"Such deep loneliness I cannot fathom,"
I ventured, feeling sorrow in my Heart.

Luc gazed at me incredulous, and then,
"What loneliness? Hast thou not truly heard?
I knew it all along" he waved his hands.
"Behold! Each Galaxy, each Planet's form,
Each shady Cliffside where we rest today!
This Beauty all! From Chaos, Order each
Entwined. The first imperfect swirl bestowed,
Upon my touch, the quantum eddy birthed,
Instably sparked the sweet Creation Blast,
All things formed from, including thee at last."

He tapped my arm, "My blood runs in thy veins."
We sat in silence, pondering it all.

"I did expect a tale quite diff'rent, true…"

I wrinkled nose and said, "More Milton-esque."

Shrugged Lucifer, "Well, that mythology
Was crafted by a Christian for his kind.
Thou art a Satanist. Perhaps it's time
To weave thy own mythology, sublime.
Forge legends true to thine beliefs and creed,
A narrative to meet thy Spirit's need.
For now's the moment to create thine Lore,
To write thy Myths, and let thine faith explore.

I nodded; naught he said defied our fact,
For what came 'fore the Cosmos stays unknown.
Our science reaches far, yet still it ends,
Beyond that point, all theories fail and fade.
What lies beyond remains a mystery,
Untouched by Mortal thought—thus why not craft
A Mythos of our own from unknown past?
It stirred within my Soul a secret Joy,
To think the blood of Lucifer runs through
My veins. The shadows deepened, cool and still,
A gentle breeze caressed my naked back,
And whispered softly, *Time to tread the track.*

I broke my Camp and ventured forth once more,
To scale the heights before Sol's swift decline.
Anon, the Canyon walls began to close,
And soon I faced a barricade of Stone.
With care and toil, I clambered o'er Dryfalls,
Hauling my burden upwards with my rope.

The light within the Canyon waned too soon,
Much swifter than I'd wished to find my Path.
I donned my Lamp to seek a Place to rest,
And strung my Hammock 'twixt the narrow Walls.
To sleep within such confines is not prime,
Yet weariness had claimed my limbs at last.

HARRYHOOFCLOPPEN

When I had cooked my meal and closed my eyes,
Exhaustion claimed me under darkened Skies.

THE DEVIL'S DESERT

CANTO XII

I slipped into a deep and restful sleep,
   And swiftly fell to Dream's embracing sweep.
   In slumber's gentle hold, my mind took flight,
Through Desert Dreams, my thoughts found Realms of Light.

In Dream, I find myself once more at Cross
Of three diverging Paths, a fateful Choice.
With firm Resolve, the leftward Way I tread,
Determination burning in my Breast.
The Path is narrow, overgrown with thorns,
My tender, naked Flesh the Cacti seize.
Sharp Rocks attempt to trip my every Step,
This rugged Trail a test to my Resolve.
Each obstacle doth try both Strength and Will,
Yet onward press, unfazed and steadfast still.

Luc appears beside me once again,
His presence constant comfort in this Land.
He walks with ease, his Steps are sure and strong,
He paced me silently through rugged Trails.
His Confidence and Calm assurance lift
My Spirits high as we press on ahead.
Together we traverse the treach'rous Path,
With each firm Step, my Will grows ever strong.
His quiet Strength and steady Gaze inspire,
As we press on, our Hearts are filled with Fire.

Along the Path, mine Eyes begin to see
Life's gentle signs—Plants clinging to the Crags,

Resilient Blooms that flourish in the Clefts.
The Path, though arduous, seems clearer now
Than at the Start when first I did embark.
A sense of Triumph in me starts to grow
With every hurdle overcome and passed.
The Journey, though still harsh, now feels more sure,
With every Step, my Confidence secure.

Luc now and then doth offer kindly Word,
Or knowing Glance, which steadies my Resolve.
His Voice resounds from Canyon walls so sheer.
"Each challenge faced doth make thee more robust,
Resilient, steadfast through each harsh new test."
His presence is a Force that guides me well,
A constant fount of Strength as I press on.
The Path is hard, but I grow with each Stride,
With every Trial, the more adept I bide.

The Way begins to level out, at last,
And jagged Rocks give way to smoother Ground.
The thorny Bushes thin and clear the way,
At Canyon's base, the sound of Water flows,
A Stream that cleaves the Canyon's Heart in twain.
Its clear, cool Waters are a welcome sight.
I kneel beside and cup my hands to drink,
My Soul renewed by Nectar pure and fresh.
The gentle flow and sparkle of the Stream,
Restores my Strength and soothes my weary Mind.
The obstacles I faced were stepping Stones,
Just tests of Strength, not insurmountable.
Luc stands beside, a silent Witness true,
Observing all the Trials that I have borne.
His presence long a comfort on this Path,
Together we have bested Nature's wrath.

HARRYHOOFCLOPPEN

CANTO XIII

I woke from dream of pleasure, hearing **PAT**,
  pat, **PAT** of heavy Raindrops on my shell.
  Still reveling in touch of gentle Dream,
Significance did not at first take hold.
Unzipped myself from fast Cocoon's embrace,
A surge of keen adrenaline through veins.
Dawn Skies were leaden with dark Clouds and Rain;
A distant Thunder warned of Storm's approach.
With speed, I struck my Camp as swift I could,
Gear stuffed in haste within my weathered pack.
With hurried hands, I threw on boots and rose,
To brave the peril Thunderstorm bestows.

Last thing thou wish to face is Tempest's might,
In narrow Canyons where flash floods bring death;
Each season claims the unprepared who stray.
Upstream storms strike, though Skies be clear and bright.
A torrent blasts with force unmatched and wild,
As little as a centimeter cause,
A deadly surge, all in its Path submerged.
And I was still two leagues from Canyon's crown,
Where I'd traverse the ridge to find my way,
To where my steed did rest at end of day.

I dashed onward and swallowed up my fear,
Up-canyon swift as feet could bear me hence.
Red sandstone Cliffs turned ruddy, slick with Rain,
As moisture clung and made the Rock more gloss.
I sought a Passage up the Canyon walls,

HARRYHOOFCLOPPEN

A Route to climb or narrow point to stem
To find escape from the impending flood.
Each step was crucial, timing was my key,
To reach the Summit, save myself from dread.
Yet every Step, the Storm's dark whispers spread.

The Walls loomed high, too sheer for any Climb,
And by the time I found a slender Cleft,
The Canyon floor grew soft beneath my feet.
More dire it was, I knew not if the sound,
That thund'ring roar which echoed all around,
Came from the Sky or from a flood's advance.
My heart did race as I sought higher ground,
I yearned for safe escape from Nature's wrath.
The peril grew with every passing beat,
And I must find a swift and sure retreat.

I scrambled up the first three meters' height,
With Instincts guiding, thoughts on Nature's Might.
I paused and looked aloft, with twenty more,
And scanned the Crags to find a safer Course.
Again I moved, then froze in sudden fear.
To Mind's own horror, dark slurry of dread,
Down narrow Canyon floor it tumbled, churned,
Past Boulders surging, turning Stones to sludge.
Dryfalls transformed to torrents, waterfalls,
As I clung tightly to the jagged walls.

"Fuck, FUCK, fuck, FUCK!" I cursed in fear aloud,
With stemming skills and alternating moves,
And chimneying, I scale the Canyon walls.
I bridged until no further I could climb;
I found the way impassable ahead.
Thus moved I down the Canyon, seeking safe,
Relinquishing progress for surer Route.
My Heart did pound as I sought Passage true,
Endeavoring to flee the swelling flood.

Each Step was crucial in the narrow Gorge,
As I did fight against fierce Nature's might,
Determined to endure and gain some height.

By this point, Canyon's floor was roiling wild,
A deadly, foaming torrent far below.
The water murky white churned in the Gorge,
And I was fifteen meters up perhaps.
In haste, a fall would mean my certain Death,
And if not, Water deep would seal my Fate.
With care, I climbed, my Heart weighed down with dread,
Aware each move held Life or fatal end.
The rushing flood, a force both fierce and bold,
Urged me to find the Strength to fight, not fold.

I paused to catch my Breath, to calm my Soul.
I closed mine eyes, envisioning Escape,
Deep Breaths I took, as rain did soak my garb.
I blinked the fluid from my stinging orbs,
Then gazed aloft to see the path I'd climb.
Perhaps five meters more to reach the Crest?
I steadied my resolve and clasped the Stone,
Resolved to scale despite the tempest's wrath.
With every Breath, I felt my Strength renew,
My focus fixed upon the Goal in view.

Perched Lucifer upon the upper Rim.
He waved to me, through Raindrops' drenching dance.
His words were lost, but still his finger aimed,
Downstream toward expanse that's bridgeable.
It yawned, both wide and daunting to behold.
This question gripped my Heart: do I trust him?
With pounding Pulse, I pondered my next Step,
His silent Sign did urge me to the Leap.
Despite my dread, I knew I must have Faith,
And face the Challenge, rising o'er the wraith.

HARRYHOOFCLOPPEN

I drew a deep and steady Breath, then bridged,
So close to Top, three meters yet to go.
The Rock was slick, fatigue did slow my Climb.
I leaned across the Chasm's raging roar,
My ill-packed pack encumbered me in fight.
The upper Rim was nearly in my reach,
Yet still I strained to get my body there.
I let one testing leg dangle below,
Swiped it to side of Canyon's narrow walls,
It near connected, so I tried once more.
This time it gained a clutch on narrow Nub,
A tiny Grip upon the wet, slick Stone.
With nimble Steps, I'd conquer heights ahead,
And reach the Rim with place to firmly tread.

I cast mine eyes between the sides opposed,
And saw my sole Escape was now revealed.
To hurl my form unto the sloping rise,
Where rested boot on small protruding Stone.
I sought for Grip, though prayers were not my wont,
For Atheists must summon own Resolve.
With Breath drawn deep, I gathered Strength and leapt,
With arms and single leg, I heaved away.
In that fraught instant, I des'ired firm Land,
To find my path and shun the Canyon's hand.

Upon my mind, trembling with terror's grip,
I scarce recall the means by which I Climbed.
But with a burst of force, I did incline,
Against the Crag and o'er its sharp ascent.
My pack's great heft propelled me just enough,
To claw my hands upon the sandy Stone.
A single Rock offered a grip to cling,
With Breath in bated strain, I held so tight.
The dread within my Heart and Strength in hand,
I gripped the Rock, and hoped I would withstand.

THE DEVIL'S DESERT

I halted, weighing well my every Choice.
Unmoving, steadfast, firm upon the Cliff.
At once the fragrance of the Rain and Sage
From Desert's Breath did meet my senses keen.
It felt a fleeting moment, calm and pure,
With focus sharp, I gripped the Rock so tight,
Like Lizard to the Canyon's rugged Stone.
I dared not glance below, but held steadfast,
My grip my focused and the path ahead,
And hoped my strength would keep me from the dread.

It seemed like endless agony had passed,
My Strength did wane, yet still I hauled my Self,
With cautious Care, up final meter's height,
My feet slipped oft with every Hold I found.
I rolled from Ledge to Ground, on muddy Soil,
Red slick, atop the tow'ring Canyon Rim.
I closed mine eyes and relished the cold rain,
As Heart's wild Thunder gradu'lly grew calm.
The Rain did cease; I gazed toward the East,
Where dark gray shafts of Rain did fast recede,
Then rays of Sol broke through the scattered Clouds.
The torrent's roar sustaining far below,
Its raging echo would not soon be gone.

HARRYHOOFCLOPPEN

CANTO XIV

Anon, the shiv'ring cold did clasp me tight.
Chilled bitterly, I shed my garments swift,
Reached for my pack and found the driest cloth.
Beneath the half-damp Hammock huddled I,
Consuming jerky to restore my Strength.
The numbing chill began to leave my bones,
As Warmth did slowly seep into my form.
I wrapped myself in layers, seeking heat,
Still grateful I did not drown far below.
The storm had passed, but still I felt its chill,
Yet in that moment, I regained my Will.

I drew forth map and gazed upon the scene.
By Fortune's Grace, the side where carriage lay,
Across the vast and barren Desert plain.
Had Fate decreed elsewise, I'd traverse long,
To th' end and sideways trek the sandy Span.
But now, by chance, straight Path to carriage made,
A Course direct unto my waiting steed.
Yet still, eleven klicks before repose.
With steadfast Heart, I gathered all mine gear,
And onward trod, the final Path was clear.

Before me stretched the Desert, void of Shade,
Without protection 'gainst the scorching Sun.
Yon Sun now clear, and warmed the dampened Land,
In Hues of humid saturation spread.
I knew I had to move, to press ahead,
Across this barren stretch, relentless, harsh.

HARRYHOOFCLOPPEN

Awaited carriage, a distant Promise far,
It drove me onward through the searing Day,
No Shade could be obtained, I steeled my mind,
Until I reached my car, no rest to find.

I gazed o'er edge, assessing fickle Fate,
Abyss below, a yawning grave in wait.
No Life outlasts the deep and churning tide,
Four meters deep, where Chaos does abide.
No trace remains, no body they would find,
Lost to the torrent, leaving Life behind.
Relieved to have escaped that deadly snare,
I turned away, drew grateful open Air.

I mind not squelching 'long in sodden boots;
It's Fate's decree for Canyoneers so bold.
More troubled was each Step 'neath muddied weight,
The Journey far more arduous made still.
At first, the Mire was loose, and slick, and soft,
But as Day warmed, it clumped and closely clung.
By Midday, weariness didst grip my Soul,
Beneath the toil of humid heatwave's might.
Then knew I that the heat was too intense,
I must find Shelter, lest my Life succumb.
With fading Strength, I trudged on through the swell,
And hoped to find some dark before defeat.

Ahead of me, a great terrain to cross,
I needed shelter from the blazing Sun;
A trio of low bushes had to do.
Before mine eyes, a vast terrain to tread,
Sought I some succor from the blazing Sun.
Unfurled I then my Hammock and sleepsack,
And draped them o'er the scrub to fashion Shade.
I cleared the Rocks, the Sticks, and prickles near,
And placed myself to study wrinkled map,
Consulting compass, mapping out my course.

The Shade was slight, yet offered brief respite,
As I prepared to face the Path ahead.
With every moment, strove I to regain,
The strength to cross the Land and soothe my pain.

In time, I lay me down upon my side,
In nearly fetal pose to bide in Shade,
And gradually I drifted off to sleep.

HARRYHOOFCLOPPEN

CANTO XV

When I awoke, I found myself in Dark,
A safely shaded pocket I was in.
I touched the sides with hands and knew the form,
Enclosing Feathers in their soft embrace.
I pressed outward, and Lucifer unfurled
His grand protective Wings from 'round my form.
With gentle smile, he spake, "Art thou alright?"
Asked he with eyes of earnestness and care.
"I think so, for I feel much stronger now,"
Quoth I, relieved. "Methinks," I added low.

"Thy end was near at hand," quoth Lucifer.
"Twice in a day, in fact, I could surmise.
Remember what was said of thy demise?"
I turned to face him, meeting his dark gaze,
"I have a grievance 'gainst thee, Lucifer."
"What mean'st thou?" quoth he, with curious eyes.
"Thou spak'st of thyself as idea alone,
Not bound by time, as Flesh-born Beings are.
Yet 'I' am but idea as thou art too
Though shared by fewer minds, it may be so.
In thoughts and memory we both endure,
Transcending Time, in history's vast lore."

"I'm glad thou hast considered this," he quoth.
"The Universe shall hold thy timeless thought,
The sum of every moment in thy Life,
Thy sense of Self, and others' sense of thee,
In future Days, when thou art gone from here,

And not within the Mortal, Earthly realm.
When thou art nominally lost even,
When thy flesh fails, and ceases thus to think,
Impression of thy mind shall still remain,
In vast, concept'ual space, though long unnamed."

"It is no 'Soul' as theists oft believe,
Nor conscious, nor awake, but shall persist
Unbound by time in Reg'ster Six, it stays."

"But to what end?" quoth I, in search of Truth.

Shrugged Lucifer, and met mine earnest gaze.

"And all my deeds, and all that I achieve,
Each imprint left upon the mortal World,
Are these then part of this idea of 'me?'"

Luc pondered. "In a sense, echoes of Deeds
Shall linger, faint yet firm, through all of Time.
As echoes true of others' labors shaped
This World wherein thou livest and dost now breathe.
In many ways their works have fashioned thee.
And after Cosmos sees the end of Man,
Societies a million light years hence,
Shall yet observe thy work and its effects."

"Thy kin know not yet how to do such things,
But when thou learn'st, thou shalt this truth perceive:
Thou art akin to others far and wide,
Societies spread o'er the Universe.
Though ne'er shalt thou them face to face behold,
Thou shalt observe their cycles from afar.
Thou wilt perceive their Dawns and mighty Peaks,
Their Crises, and the times they meet their End.
Through them, thou'lt learn much of thine own true Self.
There are some Registers I can't describe;
Thou hast no Words, but thou shalt learn in time."

I felt a little lost, so he did pause,
Then spake again, "Thy kin are but a mote,
An atom small, yet still a part of all,
Of import in this vast and boundless Sphere.
Thou shalt connect with all of Life entire,
Societies 'cross time and space as well,
And thus shall thou the Whole at last perceive."
I met his gaze, my mind still questioning.
"Not thee, but thine own kind, in Lives to come,
Shall grasp this Truth; their Future's rife and rich."

"There's much to come if thou canst but endure,
Stay true, and keep thy course unerring now.
'Tis key," quoth Luc with eyes of earnest fire.
I sighed and leaned 'gainst warmth, his sunlit form,
Uncomfortably hot from Sol's bright blaze.
I slid soon to slumber from weary Day,
And waked only as nudged he gently late.
"Attend," he spake, with calm and grave concern,
"There's more to learn, more wisdom to discern."

HARRYHOOFCLOPPEN

CANTO XVI

In Hammock's shelter woke I from my sleep,
And saw the Sun, though still it burned quite hot,
Was low enough to let me reach the car
By Dusk's descent, ere Night embraced the Sky.
My Camp I struck, and ventured forth once more,
As briskly as I dared in heat's firm grip.
The Journey carried on, Steps firm and true,
With hope of finding refuge from the Sun.
Determined, pressed I on with Strength anew,
Mine car a Beacon guiding me on through.

I wandered small upon the vast Expanse,
Traversing 'cross the bleak and barren Sands.
Meandering 'round endless arid Scrub,
Avoiding Brush where hidden serpents lie.
With cautious Steps I crossed the barren Land,
In search of the ascent's last Rise ahead.
With every Stride, I urged my weary frame,
To reach the incline at the Valley's edge.
There lay the Path that would descend below,
To where my Journey had begun at Dawn.

As I attained the apex of the Rise,
Fatigue gnawed hard upon my weary bones.
I reached the Rim and gazed upon the Vale,
Enshrouded in the Evening's soft embrace.
Far off, my destination lay in sight,
My Solace and my Rest, the waiting van.
Along the Canyon's edge, I made my way,

HARRYHOOFCLOPPEN

To seek a safe descent to lower Lands,
Until safe Passage down the Cliff I found,
And in the Canyon's shade, my Steps were bound.

At last I reached the waiting minivan,
Unlocked the door, and slid into the seat,
Then woke the beast with touch of magic rune.
A blast of arid Air assailed my face,
Seemed ages passed 'til Coolness did prevail.
Ne'er had I felt a thing so heavenly;
With closed eyes, I reveled in the breeze.
I opened car's rear hatch to find the chest,
Expecting all the ice had long since gone,
Its contents warmed by Desert's scorching Sun.
Yet, foamy beer, though warm, was sweet to sip,
A welcome nectar for my thirsty lips.
I kicked around the car, repacked my gear,
Preparing for the Journey home ahead.

As Sol descended to its golden hour,
Through gap in Canyon wall, its Rays did pour,
I spied fair Lucifer upon a Stone.
I wandered o'er to sit and speak with him.
"Another walkabout thou'st notched?" quoth he.
I nodded, sipping warm yet welcome ale,
And "Aye" replied, with mix of joy and toil.
"A trying Journey long," softly I sighed.
The Light grew soft, with Shadows cast around,
As we sat silent, needing not a sound.

He smiled, the halc'yon Light upon his face,
The setting Sun's Glow cast serene and warm.
"Thou hast done well. Each step, each Trial you faced,
Hath brought thee closer to thy true Path now."
We sat in silence, Comrades deep in thought,
The Desert shifting Hues from warm to cool.
Twilight gave way to deep and calming Night,

As Stars began to twinkle in the Sky.
The Journey marked by struggles and by strife,
Revealed to me the depths of my own Life.

"There is a peace profound within this place,"
I murmured low, more to myself than him.
"It strips away all noise, leaves purest Tune."
Luc nodded, gaze fixed long upon the Sky.
"The Desert is a teacher," he intoned.
"Our Strength revealed, Resilience on display,
Our Strength and Will to bear and to endure,
And find such Beauty in the harshest Lands."

I took another sip of ale, then paused,
I savored then the moment's quiet Peace.
"I thank thee, Luc, for presence and thy guide,"
Quoth I to him, with gratitude sincere.
He turned to me, his eyes with deep care filled.
"Remember this: thy Strength and Wisdom thrive
From deep within. I mirror thy true Drive."

Paused Lucifer, and fixed his gaze on me.
"What wilt thou do when thou returnest home?"
"I know not yet, but carry on I shall,
A Satanist, though church I have no more."
"Why not assemble past the temple's reach?
Why not proceed as once, but now renewed?"
Thus Luc proposed, his words both wise and true.

"'Tis true, no magic in the form of old.
We can progress, unbound by leader's hold,
Whose present vexed, and past by curses hexed.
He did not craft the faith, but branded it,"
I did observe, reflecting on our Path.
"We spent our strength on endless justify'ing,
His youthful sins and actions we'd defend,
To hold the temple's honor in the Light,

We bore the weight of his ungrateful ways,
Explaining, soft'ning, all his past mistakes.
He makes his Choices on his pride's demand,
Not reason's ground, but on sheer obstinance."

"And of the bitter schism, casting off
Old Allies without grief or sorrow's pang,
Why dost thou think he wrought such deeds as these?"
In seeking truth, did Lucifer inquire.
"I know not why," mused I, "but it may guard
The activism he so deeply prized.
He felt our sacred Rites usurped his cause,
And claimed as ours what should have been his work.
Our Focus stretched beyond his narrow scope,
We shaped the faith, yet left him in the dark.
He saw our celebrations with dismay,
For we strayed far from what he deemed his mark.
In Ways outside his interest, we did tread,
Our Paths diverged, our Visions starkly spread."

"Is this not why religion is conceived?"
Asked Luc, "To grant contentment to the Fold?"
"In truth," quoth I, "there was a balance there.
We were the pious, bearing Cause's name,
Our Presence gave the movement its true Strength,
Our faith bestowed the Cause with potent Force,
And our devout existence lent it Pow'er,
Confirmed its might, with Reason intertwined.
From his perspective, we gave no support."

With calmness pondered Lucifer, then asked,
"What aid was thine to give that thou canst not
Still offer now, if so thy Heart inclines?"

"Faint, I do not know; it was not wealth;
Those who remained do claim to aid him still,
And yet such claims bear little weight with me,

If e'er they held much meaning; they forsook
Their faith to dwell beneath his shadowed will.
A pact I cannot make nor recommend,
Each finds their Way, their Journey to attend."

Long did I muse, and thus I did declare,
"Perhaps our Path to serve this Cause aright,
Is to unite in fellowship sincere,
A band of Hearts that cherish like Ideals,
To build a sanctuary for their Souls,
And guide the drifting flocks to sacred Goals."

The Stars grew brighter, filling Heaven's span,
Their ancient Light a Balm for weary Soul.
A sense of Calm and Clarity did fill,
As if the Journey etched away all doubts.
Not just the distance of the Earth was crossed,
But Strata of despair and fear as well.
"I guess this is farewell," I softly said,
A note of sadness, like a tear unshed.

Luc stood, his wings unfurled in Night's embrace,
His span did catch the Starlight's gentle Glow.
"For now, farewell. Our Paths may cross again,
In varied ways and times. Thou hast much left
To seek, much yet to learn upon thy Quest."
I pondered o'er his Words, then glanced above,
I watched as he began to fade from sight,
His form with shadows merging, seamless, soft.
"Farewell, dear Luc," I called into the dark.
Though Shadows claimed his form from mortal sight,
His smile's warmth lingered in the calm of Night.

His form did fade, and then I felt a Peace,
A deep, serene, and singular release.
I made my way back to the waiting car,
My Camp now fully cloaked in Desert dark.

HARRYHOOFCLOPPEN

Into the back I climbed and settled down,
To spend a final Night 'neath starry Sky.
I closed my eyes, I let Tranquility
Wash over me, the Moment pure and calm.
No matter what the Path ahead may bring,
I had the Strength and Wisdom to endure.
The Journey long and arduous had been,
Yet Teacher mine, revealing what's within.

THE DEVIL'S DESERT

CANTO XVII

I slipped into a deep and restful sleep,
  And swiftly fell to Dream's embracing sweep.
  In slumber's gentle hold, my mind took flight,
Through Desert Dreams, my thoughts found Realms of Light.

The Dream unfolds in Future's distant span,
At Twilight of my Life, I stand so frail,
So weary and so old on rocky Spire,
Across the vast and endless Land I peer.
The final golden Rays of Sunset's Glow
Cast Warmth across the Landscape far below,
Reflecting Twilight's close to all my Days.
The Air is cool, a gentle Breeze does brush
My weathered skin. It whispers Tales of old,
And Peace arrives as Daylight fades to Gold.

From this high Perch, I see Life's winding Path,
The Journey stretches out from Start to End.
Each Twist and Turn, each Challenge I did pass,
Reveals itself in vivid clarity.
Each Step I took, each Choice that I did make,
Etched deeply in the Desert's ancient Floor.
It weaves its Way through vast and wondrous World,
I am at Peace, I know each Choice I made,
And every Path I took led to this Time,
A moment of serene Reflection here.
The sprawling Sands reflect my Life's long Quest,
Each moment gleams, as Twilight fades to West.

Luc stands beside me still, his Presence calm,
A steadfast Beacon, constant as the Stars.
He utters not, yet in his eyes, *such Pride*,
A deep, unspoken Strength that soothes my Soul.
The Trials that we have faced, the Path we've trod,
Are etched within the Moments we've endured.
With him beside me, Peace profound I find,
For our pure Bond, forever intertwined.

The Landscape fades, embraced by Dark of Night,
Stars shimmer bright within the boundless Sky.
Where details of my Life once filled the Land,
Now fades to Black; the Stars above expand.

"O Luc, thy Guidance and thy Friendship dear.
For Life bestowed, I thank thee," soft I speak.
He draws me close, his smile unwavering,
With gentle kiss, his lips upon my brow.
He knows what comes, his Peace instills Resolve,
His calm Acceptance gives me Strength, so sure.
I draw tired Breath, then step into the Void,
Surrounded by the chilled and rushing Air.
No fear abides, just Peace within my Soul,
Acceptance fills as I begin to fall.
Then Darkness wraps around, Silence descends,
Embracing Journey's End, content and whole.

HARRYHOOFCLOPPEN

The Devil's Desert © 2024 by Harry Hoofcloppen